My Past Decisions Have Made Me Who I Am Today

A MEMOIR

ELLA WHITAKER

BLUEPRINT PRESS
INTERNATIONALE

My Past Decisions Have Made Me Who I Am Today
Copyright © 2023 by Ella Whitaker

ISBN
978-1-961117-16-7 (Paperback)
978-1-961117-17-4 (eBook)
978-1-961117-15-0 (Hardcover)

THIS BOOK IS dedicated to my dad's father and my two daughters. I am very thankful that God chose them to help shape my life. My grandfather introduced me to Jesus Christ when I was in my teenage years. God used my grandfather as an instrument to form my foundation. I willfully gave my life to Jesus Christ when I was a teen. Thank you, Grandfather, for obeying God. My daughters were my reason for putting one foot in front of the other. They made my life worth living. My oldest daughter gave me a Scripture about ten years ago that changed my life. This Scripture is from the Amplified Version of the Bible. It says, "I do not consider, brethren, I have captured and made it my own yet; but one thing I do (it is my one aspiration): forgetting what lies behind and straining forward to what lies ahead" (Phil. 3:13).

To me, this Scripture says your past life is finished. From my past, I got what I needed to propel me into the future. My power and my strength originated from my past. I am not there yet, but I am not where I used to be. I am going to enjoy where I am, on the way to where I'm going.

As the deer panteth for the water so my soul longeth after Thee. You are my heart's desire, and I long to worship Thee. You alone are my strength my shield. You alone may my spirit yield. I had and have an intense longing for God. I have come from longing and regret to perplexity, then to trust and assurance. Jesus you're my friend and you are my brother, even though you are a King. I love you more than any other, so much more than anything.

(Psalm 42) The King James Version.

TABLE OF CONTENTS

INTRODUCTION

WHEN I WAS growing up, I thought I was unhappy and unfulfilled, until I was married for the first time. What a rude awakening! My husband later committed suicide, and I almost lost my mind. A friend at the time could see that I needed some help, so she referred me to a person who could help me with inner healing. The hope was that this could help me deal with my grief and trauma. This all took place in the early 1980s. I was thirty years old when my husband died.

This person told me that I needed to share with others—in book form—what I had shared with her about my life. After hearing this, I had to ponder it. At that time, I didn't share too much of anything pertaining to my life with anyone.

I prayed about it, because she thought I could be healed and also help other people at the same time. I love helping others; I felt like this was what I was supposed to do—write a memoir. Still, it was very hard to get started. The wounds that had occurred in my life were open and bleeding, and the pain was almost unbearable. I was depressed, afraid, to the point of a nervous breakdown. I couldn't write what I wanted to express on paper; it hurt too much. So I tried recording it on tape, but that didn't work either; I was crying too much. I really didn't want to deal with the pain.

Each year, from the early 1980s to 2012, I would write some things down on paper until my emotions got the best of me. At that point, I would stop writing. My emotions improved each year, because my mind and body were being healed by the act of writing the small section I was able to write.

I have so much more to add to the book, more tragedy and healing over the course of thirty-two years that will be shared in these pages. I don't reflect on those bad times in my mind anymore; it was, at one time, constant in my mind, and I had no peace. By finishing this book, I have my past in the open now, and it feels good. I feel free at last from my past, by the grace of God.

CHAPTER 1

I AM WRITING this book for several reasons. The first is my need to heal from past hurts. Writing it on paper has healed a lot. The second reason is my hope that it might help others to overcome some obstacles in their lives.

I was born in 1946 in a small town in Texas. I am the oldest of four kids, one sister and two brothers. I am two years old older than my sister, four and a half years older than my first brother, and eight and a half years older than my baby brother. As such, I was like a second mother to them.

I was a quiet kid with deep thoughts. I attended a small elementary school in a rural area for eight years, first grade through eighth. High school was located within the town's city limits. I graduated in 1965 at the age of eighteen.

My perception of my early years was that I was not a happy camper. Most of those eighteen years were lived in a rural area six miles outside of the small town. The place wasn't bad, just remote. My parents owned the land we lived on, which was a blessing.

I learned how to drive at age fourteen, courtesy of a crash course while driving my dad. He had picked me up from my aunt's house one night, and he was very intoxicated. I told him I wasn't going to ride with him in that condition, so he said, "You drive." So I did. I drove in second gear all the way home, which was about four miles. After that, I was an automobile driver; I knew how to drive, so I could leave the country—which is what we called the rural area where we lived.

I seldom had access to the car. My dad would leave home on Friday evenings, and we might not see him again until Sunday evening. So the rest of the family was stuck at home, for the most part, and that was depressing.

I played basketball in high school, as well as community softball, volleyball, and football. I was a tomboy, and playing ball was a release for me. My mother wanted me to excel in school, and I did. I made the honor roll in high school. But I was lonely, and I didn't talk much. I observed a lot and listened.

I had a lot of responsibilities, being the oldest. We had no running water in the house; we had an outhouse, and we had a wood stove for heat and a gas cooking stove, which I was afraid of. I made the house shake one morning. My sister and I had to cook breakfast every morning for our dad. This particular morning, I had turned the oven on and made the biscuit dough. I thought the oven was on, but it wasn't; the pilot light was out. When I discovered this, I lit a match. I didn't think about how much time had passed before I discovered the pilot light was out. I was blown backward, and the sound woke everybody up. I once asked my mom, "Why don't you cook breakfast for your husband?" My thoughts were I would use that time to prepare for school. That question didn't go over very well.

My dad wanted me to excel in sports; my mother wanted me to excel in school. I tried to please both of them. My mother programmed me during those eighteen years I was at home. I was to take care of her. I don't believe she knew that she was developing me to be an enabler for her. When I got older, I found out what the word *enabler* meant.

So at age eighteen, I was an enabler. *How does one change this?* I asked myself. That was all I knew how to be at that time. I was also ridiculed a lot. When things didn't go the way Mom wanted with Dad, I got the blame. At those times, she saw me as the enemy it seemed to me. I would sometimes get smacked across the face, and she'd tell me, "You are so much like your dad's relatives!" I don't remember the reason for the smack, other than the fact that I was the daughter of her husband.

I loved my mother very much, but I didn't feel loved by her. That's not to say that she didn't love me; she did. She just didn't know how to express it, from my perspective. Each person in the family has different perspectives, about their life in the same household; we just filter things out differently. She would ridicule me and not realize it.

My mother was the product of her environment. She had issues from her childhood, like most of us do. I was treated much better by her than she had been by her mother. I was trying to please my mother, and my dad just wanted to be away from us much of the time.

From my observations, my mom didn't feel love from her mother, though she knew her mother loved her. There is such a wide contrast between knowing and showing.

My mother was very strong in her convinced way of thinking, not to say that her thinking was right or wrong, either way, right or wrong, what you say will work for you. What you say is very powerful, and you will have what you say if you don't doubt, Says Jesus Christ.

I was very twisted, because of my environment.

My parents were not very good role models for me when it came to marriage. I didn't actually see any role models in the community. Everyone seemed unhappy. They all seemed to be alcoholics; that was their release.

CHAPTER 2

MY PARENTS DIDN'T take us to church as a family, until homecoming Sunday. That happened once a year. The family would go to church on this Sunday before the revival week. When I was eight or nine years old, we lived near a church that I could walk to, I would attend Sunday school. I was fascinated by the preacher when he was preaching, I listened, and I paid attention while the other kids would talk and pass notes to each other.

This place where we lived was a lumberyard. There were several families living in the lumberyard. When I was ten or eleven, we moved to the land Mom and Dad had bought. We went from faucet water, which was placed in the center of the yard for all the families in the lumberyard to use, to getting our water from a well.

My dad showed me that the man should work; he had a job. Of course, what he did with the money from that job is a different story. We never went hungry at home; there was always something to eat. We always had a garden, and we would go fishing. Dad had pigs, and he and my brothers would go hunting, so we had wild animals also to eat. We had chickens, nasty chickens. I didn't like those nasty chickens; they were not friendly to the yard, and we had two dogs.

When we moved onto our land, my dad had to dig a well for us to acquire water to live on. Being the oldest of the kids, I had some hard chores to do. I had to draw water from the well and make a fire around the pot, a big, black, iron object we used to heat the water for washing clothes. Just the act of washing clothes was a big chore. Nobody really had a weight problem back then, like people do now, because we were always outside doing physical exercise. We played a lot of cowboys and Indians games and physical sports. I had lots of cousins; they were like sisters and brothers to me. Having them in my life made life bearable, at the most loneliest time.

CHAPTER 3

MY DAD'S FATHER was very gifted with words; he knew the Bible. But from what I could see, he didn't live the talk. My grandfather introduced me to Jesus Christ, and I am very grateful for that. He was an instrument from God for me, an inspiration to me regarding Jesus in my life. He would come to our home every Saturday morning and tell me to go get the Bible, so we could read. There were words I couldn't pronounce, but he could pronounce them. I would ask him how he knew the words, because he only had a third-grade education. He said God taught him how to read. I was learning a lot from him.

I started asking him questions about his deeds in life. He said that it is not what goes *into your body* that will defile you; it is what comes *out of you* that will defile you. I chewed on that for a very long time.

I took life very seriously. I didn't have much playtime because I had to take care of my siblings and my mother most of the time. She was usually depressed—angry, unhappy, and discontented. Grandmother, my mother's mother, lived right behind us, and was always coming in our back door making demands. That was unpleasant; she was a very mean woman, and she was the product of her environment. Her dad was a Cherokee Indian who had five daughters, no boys.

I learned to be disciplined in my childhood, to be in control, but I was very tight, tense, and stressed. I had no "wiggle room." I was groomed to be an enabler, but my parents didn't even realize this. I was thrust into the adult world, trying to fix people and trying to make things happen for other people, rather than making things happen for me. I was irresponsible toward myself. I was trying to make people happy and content and make them the best they could be. Not knowing how to say *no,* the only words I knew were *okay, I guess so,* and *if you want me to.*

It took me many years to learn to set boundaries and say *no.* Growing up, my happiest times were when I was playing basketball or softball and studying my lessons for school. Once a year, at Christmastime, I allowed myself to be a happy camper. Everyone seemed so glad and joyful. Mom was smiling, and Mom and Dad seemed to like each other. The house smelled like apples and oranges, and we had a pine tree for a Christmas tree. I still like the smell of pine at Christmas.

Usually, if my mother was happy and content, the kids were too; she set the stage for everyday living. Mom did what used to be called maid work, cleaning houses for other families. When she couldn't go to work because of sickness, or if school was out for the summer, I was told I had to go to work in her place. I would have to miss school that day, if school was still in session. I surely didn't like that; it was really depressing but not all bad.

I learned to control a household of three kids, clean the house, and wash the clothes. I had the same responsibilities at home, with a little help from my sister; I had most of the duties of the house. Working for my mom, I had no monetary compensation. I had the feeling of being used; I felt disappointment and confusion with no explanation why. I think I knew the reason deep down, but I sometimes wanted to hear the words spoken, and I would probably have felt appreciated. I began working at my mom's job when I was in middle school, eighth grade.

CHAPTER 4

MY ELEMENTARY SCHOOL consisted of three classrooms, a library, and a kitchen. I was hungry most of the time at school, as I had no lunch money. A nickel would have helped in high school; at least I could buy a candy bar.

In elementary school, we were given government cheese or peanut butter and crackers if we were hungry and didn't have lunch money. Everyone was given that. I didn't like cheese, but they would run out of peanut butter really quickly, because everyone wanted peanut butter. It was embarrassing not to have lunch at school, because sometimes I didn't want to take a biscuit to school to eat. I would ask my dad for a nickel, but he wouldn't give it to me. He would say he didn't have one. Sometimes it was hard to learn on an empty stomach.

My elementary-school teachers were sort of like parents to us. They taught us, disciplined us, and even loved us. They helped the parents raise their kids back then.

Remember, this was back in the 1950s and '60s; things are a little different now in the twenty-first century.

Out in the country, we did a lot of walking to get from one place to another, which was good exercise—not like today. I loved sports. I would play shortstop in softball; to me, that was where the action was. The ball was hit to that position most of the time. So I concentrated on the ball and nothing else in life.

I would walk the railroad tracks that was below our house, and I would sometimes ask God, *Why am I here? What is my purpose here?* Because I really didn't like my life at the time. I remember telling God, *I want more than I am seeing, hearing, and feeling.*

I played basketball in high school, but I didn't have transportation to and from the games; my dad said he didn't have gas in the car to take me. There was a really nice lady in my neighborhood that was a blessing to me. She would sometimes take me to school for a game. My mother couldn't drive; she never learned how. If the basketball team went out of town, my teammate and I would stay over at the home of her aunt who lived close to the school. We did this for about three years during high school.

If my dad came to see me play basketball, I never knew it. Softball, yes; he was there because it was a sport he liked, but never Mom. My mom wanted to see me finish high school and get a job. What I learned was how to take care of her. I wanted to be a nurse as one of my desired professions, also a race-car driver, a policewoman, a nun, and a psychologist. All these professions lean toward helping others… well, all except race-car driver. Still, I often think about that occupation. Maybe in my subconscious, I wanted to run away from it all.

My dad was given a chance to try out for baseball's minor leagues, but he would've had to leave home to do that. His dad was not up for that idea at all. He didn't want my dad to leave because, in my opinion, he was possessive and selfish. So my dad was talked out of going to the tryouts to play in the minor leagues.

Dad played baseball in the community; he had a reputation for being someone to reckon with. My brothers share his ability to play baseball. By not participating in the minor-league tryouts—which probably would have developed his God-given talent—he didn't encourage my brothers to excel in their gifts also. Looking back over this, I can see how, as parents, we can influence or discourage our kids by our decisions and our actions, which in turn affects the flow of the family's talents passed down through generations.

CHAPTER 5

I REMEMBER TIMES when my parents would put me in the middle of their altercations. Mom would say, "Your dad pushed me; he said this or that to me." As I stood there listening, I thought, *I am the child. What can I do? What do I do?*

I would say to Dad, "Did you push Mom?" He would try to explain that he sometimes held Mom's hands to keep from getting hit. She would get aggressive when she was angry, so he really was protecting himself, in a way. I had the responsibility of trying to smooth things over, the best I knew how. My mother relied on me as her enabler. She was trying to stay afloat, being a wife and mother, which is not easy. I was her confidant, as well as the whipping post. I got very tired of being ridiculed by my mother growing up. I didn't see much light in my life, just a lot of darkness.

I was about eight years old when my parents took us kids to spend the night at my grandfather's house. This was my dad's father; my dad's mother died when my father was sixteen, and my grandfather remarried. So we were taken to spend the night with my grandparents, whom I love dearly. My grandfather and his siblings owned quite a bit of land that was left to them by their father, and they all lived on the land.

I'm told that my great-grandfather's estate was also known as haunted land; it was once an Indian reservation. I really didn't like visiting there without my parents. My dad would tell us scary stories from his childhood days about doors opening, lights going up and down in a tree. He said he would even throw rocks at a man with no head! Dad's mother was a Choctaw Indian; I share this information because it tells a bit about my heritage. My mother's grandfather—her mother's father—was a Cherokee Indian, and her dad's grandfather was Caucasian. This heritage is not unusual in the African American's life.

One day our parents left me and my two siblings to spend the night with my dad's parents that lived on the old Indian reservation. (My baby brother wasn't born yet.) I was in between the two of them; they were always surrounding me. I had decided not to open my eyes, so I wouldn't see anything out of the ordinary. I changed my mind, and when I did open my eyes, I saw a lady floating in the air at the entry door from the kitchen! I stared at her, but I was not afraid. She was looking at me, and she started floating toward me. Our eyes locked; she was floating right above me, smiling with a look of approval on her face, before she disappeared through the back wall.

When she was completely gone, I screamed for my grandfather. By then, the peaceful feeling I'd had was gone. My grandfather said I had a dream, but I told him I was not asleep. He stayed with us until the next morning, or at least until I went to sleep, because when I awoke the next morning, he was not in the room with us.

My siblings didn't wake up during the whole incident. I have never forgotten what happened. I've prayed to God to give me an answer to my questions. Who was she? How did she know me? The expression on her face showed that she knew me. I was thinking she was an ancestor, but I still hadn't received an answer from God.

When I moved back to Texas in 2004—fifty years after this happened—I shared this with my uncle. He said she was probably an angel. That statement worked for me; it felt right, and I haven't wondered anymore. I believe God revealed that event to me that day; I also believe there was a purpose for me to see an angel then and there. God has protected me all my life; my life could be different if he hadn't. I have made so many mistakes; God is continually giving me the chance to do better.

CHAPTER 6

WHEN I WAS eleven or twelve years old, a teenage cousin came to live with us, and he molested me. I was afraid of him. He would come to my side of the bed, put his hands under the covers, and touch me in my private areas. I would push his hands off quietly, because my sister was in the bed with me. He would make conversation with us to throw off the indication of what he was doing.

I should've screamed for my mother. I can't remember if he threatened me; I just knew that if I told, I would cause a big ruckus in the family. My parents loved him like a son. I thought he would be like my big brother, but I've learned that the ones, who live in the house with you, or close to you, are often the ones who would hurt you the most.

He left the house eventually and went to another town. I never told anyone about what he did until thirty-three years later. I was reading a book that brought back memories of it. I had put those memories in a safe place, where I wasn't conscious of them anymore; but of course, they were still there in me, causing trouble in my life.

I had somehow blocked it out, put the memory into a place where I could function. The feelings came flooding back when I was reading that book when I was about forty-five years old, and I remember crawling around on the floor, crying myself into weakness so bad that I couldn't get up off the floor. I told my sister what had happened so many years ago. I didn't know what I expected from her; I just knew it was time for me to tell her, now that it had surfaced. I needed to tell someone what had happened to me, because it would help free me. It was a secret. The reaction I got from my sister was unexpected. She wanted to know why I didn't tell. I told her I was a kid then, and I didn't know what to do. I suppose I was trying to protect everyone, and I suffered that all alone. I got no understanding or words of sympathy from my sister.

Now that I am a grown woman, I know that my cousin was a mixed-up teenager. His parents were not together, and he had nowhere to go. He died a young man. I never knew what caused his death, but I was told he was found dead in his bed. I was in my twenties when he died.

I graduated high school in 1965 and joined the air force to become a nurse, because my parents couldn't afford to send me to nursing school. There were a lot of girls joining the service back then, right out of high school. The girls who joined would be taken in waves, so I took all the tests and physical exams and had to wait for the wave of girls that I would be in.

In the meantime, I went to another town in Texas and enrolled into a trade school for dry cleaning. I worked in the cleaners for several months, and then my mom called and said that the air force was ready for me. After working for several months and getting a regular paycheck, I took a liking to that, so I decided not to go into the air force. At this point in my life, I was thinking, *I am woman, hear me roar.*

I continued to work in the cleaners, feeling my independence, being on my own. I was renting a room and living by myself. When I was a kid, my dad's family religion was Methodist, and I was sprinkled with water on my head as a child. I was now living in this new town, attending church with my family there, and I united with that church. It was a Baptist church, and I wanted to be baptized at nineteen. That was a glorious experience. I felt so close to God; I had peace and joy. I was very innocent of a lot of things, and I was a virgin.

I was singing in the choir, growing in the Lord, and enjoying my life. I was renting a room about a mile from my aunt's house. I would go visit and leave her house at night. I would sometimes walk home alone. I was not afraid to go alone; it felt like I was walking with someone. I would talk to this invisible person I felt with me. I felt safe and protected. I hope never to forget that time I spent with God, walking on that road.

CHAPTER 7

IN DECEMBER 1966 I turned 20 years old, the following year in February my grandmother asked me to travel with her to Oregon, and I said yes. Two of my mother's sisters lived there, and they wanted my grandmother to come visit, and she did not want to go alone. I had always wanted to go there because of the weather. My aunts would tell me when they came to visit us in Texas that it didn't get as hot in Oregon as it did in Texas.

My grandmother and I headed for Oregon in March 1967. Looking back over my life, I see God working—shaping and molding me to be the best I can be in him. It took three days for my grandmother and me to get to Oregon. It was a wonderful trip. I was looking at the mountains and rivers along the way, remembering my geography books that we studied in elementary school, all the pictures I had seen. Now I could see these places close up, and it was personal. That was a blessing for me to experience.

When we arrived in Oregon, it seemed too enormous for me to fathom. It actually snowed the next day, which was another treat to experience. It didn't snow much in Texas when I was growing up, and when it did, we would make ice cream out of the snow.

Both of my mom's two sisters in Oregon had a child. One had a son, and the other had a daughter. My mom's sisters were twins. In Texas, I was going to church every Sunday, singing in the choir, going to lunch after church, and mingling with church members; we would call it fellowshipping with each other. These relatives didn't attend church. I really had to adjust to this; it was different. I had thoughts like, *Do I fit in? No, I am now in a strange place, in a different part of the country, in the Northwest, a whole different culture, different climate; help me, Lord. A different-sounding language and a different type of dress.*

I was excited and afraid. I knew nothing about anything. I was from a little town in Texas, from a rural area, and I was only twenty years old, just starting to feel liberated. I had no knowledge of dating men; I actually was afraid of them.

There is a sitcom I love to watch called *The Golden Girls.* When the character of Sophia was telling a story, she would always say, "Picture it." I was not streetwise; I was naïve, gullible, and very ignorant of life's problems as a grown-up. My aunts were considered a different class of people, compared to what I was used to. I had to adjust to that; I considered myself coming from a poor class of people, working hard, constantly trying to make ends meet.

That's not to say that my relatives in Oregon didn't have the same problems; they just had more benefits and made more money at their jobs. The more money you make, the higher the cost of living. Oregon's cost of living was higher than that in Texas; therefore, the wages were higher.

I was raised around drunks and adulterers. That was their life, their philosophy, which created their attitude, actions, and results, which in turn created their life. In order to make it in the Northwest, I had to change my philosophy—or should I say, make a paradigm shift. I knew a lot about learned behavior, and I didn't like what I saw growing up. My dad drank; I would call him a functioning alcoholic. Therefore, I dislike the disease of alcoholism. It changes who you are, and that person never finds out who he really is until he stops drinking. Where there is an addiction, there is a root problem that needs to be plucked out, in order to overcome it.

I considered my mother to be a pretty woman, with light skin. That influenced how we were treated in Texas and probably other places also. We were judged and evaluated by the color of our skin. The light-skinned got better treatment than the dark-skinned. Mom had long hair, which was another plus. My dad was darker than my mom; I wanted to be light like her. My skin color is somewhere between light and dark, so I was already feeling underprivileged because of my color.

As I write, and remember the culture I grew up in, I can see how I could get stuck in tradition.

I didn't become an alcoholic, and in fact, I didn't like the taste of hard alcohol. I was married at age twenty-two to an alcoholic, to continue in the madness of my learned-behavior environment. In fact, the day I met my husband, he was drunk. I met him at a mutual friend's house. He was leaving as I was going in, and he followed me back into the house. He seemed interesting, but what did I know?

CHAPTER 8

MY MOTHER TAUGHT me about honesty. She taught me to tell the truth. "Never give up," she would say. "You can get tired, you can be worn out, but never give up." My mom instilled some standards for me to live by, and what she didn't teach me, the Holy Spirit did. I am like a bulldog once I am locked into something. I won't turn loose.

I have always had the capacity to love. I used to marvel at the fact that I could look at someone and feel love, acceptance, and compassion toward them. I would say, "Lord, you have to be on the inside of me, for me to be this way; I would like to feel rage toward someone sometimes."

I could get angry, but it would take a minute. That is to say, I can take a lot before I get angry. When I do get angry, I'm in trouble, because my health is in jeopardy, and my blood pressure goes up. At this time, I'm feeling like I could probably take no prisoners.

My husband had a drinking problem, as well as emotional, mental, and spiritual problems. He was messed up. I was used to looking at twisted men; growing up, this is all I saw—from my dad to his friends, neighbors, and uncles and cousins. My first husband was divorced. I was his second wife, and he was my first husband. He was nine years older than me and had three children from his first marriage. He used to tell me I was like a breath of fresh air to him. I still don't know exactly what that meant. Maybe he meant that I was green and innocent to the ways of the world.

I came from a different culture, from the South to the North, and life was very different. It took me about five years to really get warm in the Northwest, coming from a very warm climate.

My first husband and I have two daughters together. He died after eight and a half years of marriage, by suicide. Our second child and I were with him when he committed suicide. Anyone who has experienced living with a nonfunctioning alcoholic knows the misery I had to endure.

I felt trapped after a while. He couldn't hold down a job because of his drinking. He was a very good liar—or should I say a convincing liar—and he played around with witchcraft, which I found out only *after* his death. He was also unreliable. He would leave me standing, sometimes for hours, to be picked up from work. I was the one who had to pick up the kids from the babysitter and from school, and I had to depend on him for help to meet all of these needs.

I was a nervous wreck when it came to his driving. Normally he would drive while drinking. Every once in a while, he would remember that he needed to pick me up from work. He would always insist on driving, which would cause more stress, because I didn't want to ride with him while he was under the influence.

I was drawn to that type of madness, because that was a learned behavior. I grew up around and lived with an alcoholic. I did not become an alcoholic, but to remain in the madness, I married an alcoholic. Growing up, I felt ugly and worthless and didn't think very much of myself. I was not validated by anyone in my family. It would really have added to my life if I had been told, "You are cute or pretty or beautiful, intelligent, bright, talented, smart"; any of those words would have gone a long way in my life, even to this day.

I have looked at pictures when I was younger, and realized I was attractive and didn't know it. In my mind I thought I didn't measure up to what was pleasing to the eye.

I did not have the word *no* in my vocabulary. I had to learn how to say no. I would always feel guilty, even when I thought about saying no. Learning to say no and not feel guilty about it was a great accomplishment; it took a lot of courage to say no and to teach people how to treat me. It took me years—and I truly mean years—to teach people how to treat me the way I want to be treated, not the way they wanted to treat me.

I was told by my first husband that I was ugly and stupid. He would follow me around the house and torment me with his words when he was intoxicated. Words can be very hurtful, and once the words have been said, they can't be erased. I would receive words and actions from people, and I learned later in life that I didn't have to receive what was said to me. I could denounce it, reject it, and loose it from me.

My self-esteem was in the pits. I gained a lot of weight with my second daughter; I was about two hundred pounds with her. My husband was constantly telling me when he was intoxicated, how I reminded him of everything that he was not and wanted to be. After our second daughter was born, he continued calling me fat and ugly. He was in a lot of misery, and to this day I do not know why, because he never told me all of it. He was like Jekyll and Hyde, switching personalities from good to bad when he drank alcohol.

I was in way over my head, but I was very strong in body and spirit. Still, I was being worn down by the decisions I had made and continued making. I worked and cared for the family. My husband had a job, but he didn't go in to work much. He frequently called in with some kind of lie.

I had my beliefs; I believed God could make anything possible. I found a church home and started remembering the promise I had made to my landlady while living in Texas, that I would continue to attend church and continue to grow in the likeness of Jesus Christ. I was determined to grow my children up in the church, unlike my own childhood.

CHAPTER 9

THE CHURCH HOME was a small store front church, not many members. The girls loved going, they would tell their dad about the service. After a while I noticed he wanted to hear about the service, I encouraged him to attend; and he did. A few Sunday later he became a member, and he started carrying a pocket Bible with him everywhere he went.

He started telling his friends about his experiences, and giving them scriptures to read.

My husband would hear voices in his head, but wouldn't tell me what they were saying to him. The more he attended church, more of the voices he would hear. He was tormented day and night.

One night I was awakened by the shaking of the bed, I looked around and saw nothing out of the ordinary. I looked at him, and noticed that his body was trembling;

the bed was shaking from his tremors. I asked what was happening to him, he said, I feel like I need to pray.

I said, ok let's pray, I got out of bed to kneel with him at the bed. He had to struggle to kneel; there was a force in the room keeping him from kneeling. I put my hand on his shoulder to help assist him in getting down on his knees, because he was bobbling up and down.

We prayed and return to bed. That morning he had an appointment with his doctor, a follow up from a nervous breakdown he had several weeks earlier. I didn't understand what was happening to my husband. I am very disturbed at this point.

We are on our way to the appointment and I am driving, I hear a click noise; I asked him what was that? He said the door had clicked open, he said; slow down so I can close it back. I kept slowing until he said that's enough. I had no thoughts of him stepping out of the car.

I had almost stopped the car when he said, that's enough. He gets out of the car, we was on the interstate 5 bridge between Washington and Oregon. He started toward the side of the bridge, I tried to stop him, by grabbing his belt, and I missed the belt, but ripped his pocket off his paints. There is a river under the bridge, that has strong fast currents. He steps over the rails to the outer side of the bridge; He is holding onto the rail, I grabbed his hands to hold onto him, and pleading with him not to turn loose the rail. He said the girls and I would be better off without him. My hands are now bleeding from the struggle of him and me pulling each other across the cement pillar on the bridge. The pillar was between us, it prevented me from being pulled over the rail. He soon jerked away from me, and dropped down into the river. The current took him down the river; the only thing I would see was his hat on top of the water.

I was in shock, someone had called the authorities, there was a precinct half a block away from us.

The authorities couldn't location his body, because of the current, so we had to wait until he rose to the surface, which was four days later.

My Dad identify his body, he didn't want me to do it, because of how he looked after being in the water for four days. I was determine to see his body, in my mind, he was hit on the head when he jumped into the water, and he is somewhere with amnesia, and can't find his way back home.

At the funeral, I asked to see his body; the directors finally complied with my wishes. I needed to see if his clothes matched the pocket I had pulled off his pants. The pocket matched, I was no longer being in denial. He was covered in ice, because he was frozen after being found. What I saw of him was not a pretty picture. I made it through that incident, of seeing his body, but it interrupted the normal, as I saw it for my life time.

CHAPTER 10

MY FIRST HUSBAND had a short, unhappy life; he had no joy at all when I met him. Thinking back over our lives, I feel very sad for him; he didn't know how to move forward and let go of past hurt and pain. It is such a travesty when we don't know how to free ourselves from pain and unforgiveness.

My daughters were my reason to keep on pushing and pressing in life; they were my inspiration. God was and is my source of strength to endure. God says, "You have not, because you ask not, in Jesus' name; he abides in me and me in him." God would answer my prayers in Jesus' name. I have a lot of faith. If God said it, I believe it, and I act on it. I taught my daughters and my grandsons to pray for all things and all desires.

I very much wish that my daughters could have had an earthly father. I can't change what was, but the main revelation is that they have a heavenly Father, the Almighty Father. As a young girl, I believed God had a plan for my life. I would run, because I didn't know where that plan would lead me. I'm not running anymore, because I want peace and contentment. Have you ever felt like you knew something, but you didn't know how you knew it? A phrase I've heard in describing this feeling is, "you know that you know that you know."

It is very hard to deprogram someone after childhood pain and hurt. That is why the way you raise your children is so important. What is done or not done to kids growing up will affect them for life, good or bad. That person has to rise above it with God's help; you can't do it alone. I have come a long way; I am not where I used to be. I am going to enjoy my life now, on the way to where I am going.

Some of the negative things in my childhood still haunt me today. After my husband died, I really only grieved a little. One day, I said, "I don't have time for grieving. I have a home, cars, kids, and a job. I need to put this grieving behind me and do what needs to be done for my kids and my everyday life." With that, I put grieving on the back burner. I didn't want to hurt anymore. I was afraid to feel; it seemed so overwhelming to deal with what I was experiencing.

Oregon and Washington were separated by a bridge. I lived in Washington and worked in Oregon. It was very hard for me to cross that bridge every day, the same bridge my husband had jumped from. I am what is called a recovering enabler. I have to be careful and aware not to fall back into that addiction. Whether you know it or not, it is an addiction. I have never really wanted to be in control of anything. My analogy of being in control is driving a bus. It seems at times, I never had a chance to ride the bus as a passenger; I always found myself in the driver's seat. Remember, this is an analogy I'm trying to show, not literally driving.

I found out early in life that I was surrounding myself with needy people; they needed my strength where they were weak. Looking back, I didn't want that, but it was a learned behavior, and I was being crushed. So the more I gave, the more I was being required to give.

I had to cross the interstate bridge every day to get to work. The girls were seven and three years old when we moved from Oregon to Washington, we were in Washington six months before my husband committed suicide. My youngest daughter turned four that July, my husband died in August. She didn't really remember her dad, but the seven-year-old did. She was angry at me for not letting her go to the funeral; I thought it would be best. She felt that she could've had closure, but you know we can always say what we didn't experience would've been the thing that would have helped us.

I kept prolonging my grieving; I didn't want to go through it. I would find myself going around it, under it, over it, until I said, "I'm tired of this. I am ready to go through this." Then God stepped in and started the healing process.

After my husband died, I found out a lot of things that I hadn't known were happening with him. I found out he was messing around with witchcraft, and there were demons in my home; it's true. It made a believer out of me. I don't know how many demons were in the house, but it took about twenty years to get them out. I did not address the demons until after marrying again and the second husband had left the house. We eventually were divorced, and after that, I really started noticing the demon activity in the house.

I approached one of the deacons at my church and explained to him what was happening in my home. Two deacons came out and prayed. I didn't really see any difference, but knowing what they had done made me feel a little better. It seemed like my daughters and I were fighting demons every day. I battled for my daughters; I was determined Satan would not have my children or me. I knew that we were overcomers, and we overcome by the blood of the Lamb. My Bible tells me Jesus came to Earth so that we might have life and have it more abundantly, but I was not enjoying my everyday life. I just existed.

I was disobedient in my life; I made a lot of wrong choices based on feelings, not by what God said. I met my 2nd husband in the midst of this storm. Deep down, I guess I was looking for a distraction, something to give me an escape from what I really needed to deal with. This man wanted to marry me. I didn't know that he had ulterior motives, and I am really not knocking him for that, because I learned later that I had a motive too. I wanted someone to lean on, to take care of me, protect me, provide for me, and love me. I wanted and needed to experience this; I wanted to know what it felt like.

I was married again, and I was very messed up, but it was a distraction. At this time, my first husband had been dead a year and a half. I still only knew a little bit about life after my first husband died, which meant I was still not at ease, still gullible, in some respects still very trusting of people. I think that's one of the reasons my husband was so intrigued by me, because of the differences he saw in me, compared to what he had been used to dealing with.

CHAPTER 11

MY SECOND HUSBAND told me he was a recovering drug addict. He was working as a drug-and-alcohol counselor. Academically, he was very smart, and he was sociology major in college. He told me he would see me through all of the trials I was facing; all I had to do was lean on him. I didn't realize he was using reverse psychology on me. He liked the fact that I had two daughters, two cars, a home, and a good job. As my mom used to say, he had found a bird nest on the ground. He was so different from my first husband, he was a shock to my world system—a different shock, I should say, because my first husband also shocked my world system.

My husband saw a chance to experience what he always wanted. He told me he always wanted the white-picket-fence type of life. He already had five kids. He never really helped to raise his kids in a home where he was present 24/7. But with me, he had a chance to help me raise my two daughters in a home he lived in. He started going to church with me; he hadn't been going before we were married. He also began working in the church, and he really liked the pastor.

The pastor helped my husband with some legal problems. I told him once not to worship the pastor; he was supposed to worship God. He got to experience what I was telling him. Our pastor and his wife were killed in a car accident. My husband was devastated. After that, he was in and out of church, in and out of drug use, and causing havoc. He had so much to offer, and yet he was wasting his life.

He had issues from childhood, but he never figured out the triggers. Triggers are those little things that blindside you when you're trying to get rid of something through self effort. Then, after a while, something happens that sends you back into it. Until you find what the trigger is, you will be forever chasing the wind.

I didn't give myself a chance to heal from my first husband's death. Now, things were stacking up on me. Still not over the death of my first husband, I had accumulated more problems with this husband. Like my first husband, my second also didn't want to work. He wanted me to take care of him and, to some extent, his kids also. At this time in my life, I felt stuck. I didn't want to deal with the pain of these two marriages, so I tried to suppress it, and I learned to do it pretty well.

No one knew what I was going through, mentally, emotionally, and even physically. I would even venture to say that when I married again, I was not in my right mind.

That is not to say that I was crazy, but I was mentally ill. Just as people can get physically ill, we can also be emotionally and mentally ill. And when you are mentally and emotionally ill, it can also bring you down physically. I found myself in that predicament. I start having anxiety attacks, or as some people call them, panic attacks. I was losing my grip because of too many people relying on me, expecting and requiring things of me.

I was thirty years old when my first husband died, and at thirty-three, I found myself married again. I was starting to feel as if I was only going to live until the age of thirty-three. I was thinking a lot about dying, right about then, stemming from my first husband's death.

I went to my doctor to get some help. I wasn't sleeping, I had rapid heartbeat, and I was frightened. I felt there was no one who could help me—surely not my husband, because he was depending on me to make everything right. By this time, he was feeling pressed, because he didn't want the responsibility of caring for a helpless woman. That was frightening for him, and he couldn't stand alone.

I tried to weigh all my options, resources, and faith to make decisions. I said to myself, "Stop, not so fast. Is this adding to my life or subtracting from it? I need to think about *needs,* not *wants.* The wants will get us into trouble, and our feelings will betray us also."

My life with this husband was a bit fast, meaning we were very social. My husband was charming, and he knew how to interact with almost anyone he met.

My doctor prescribed antidepressants, telling me I was depressed. When I think back, I realize that I was unfair to this husband. I had not healed from the first marriage. People make this mistake, and we rob our partners of knowing who we really are. We bring so much baggage, and when we are emotionally and mentally unstable, we attract the same sort of person. I learned that if you are well, you will attract people who are well also.

The second marriage lasted nine and a half years. It was not all bad, looking back, because I saw God in the midst of it all, developing me, protecting me, and guiding me. So I have to call it all joy, because of who I am today. My husband taught me a lot of things I will be grateful for forever. He suggested I seek counseling with a friend of his who was a psychologist. I did go to see him for several months, for help with my grieving problem. It did help.

About six months later, I went to another psychoanalyst. This doctor determined that I had a lot of anger, and I didn't know how to say no. He gave me an object I could use to hit things, and I broke the handle off of it. I was surprised, and the doctor was surprised. I had a lot of fury. I decided I had better learn how to get a release from all of these emotions, or I could hurt someone, maybe even myself.

CHAPTER 12

MY HUSBAND SAW me getting stronger in physical strength as well as in emotional and mentally. He started to run, because he didn't know what he was doing in terms of being a husband and a father. He admitted that to me. I commend him for telling me this, because most people would never admit if they don't know what they're doing.

I continue to get stronger, with God's help. My mom always taught me never to give up. I needed all my strength to make it through each day. By this point in the marriage, my husband was draining me, and I needed peace very badly. I had concluded that my church was not there for me; it was just me and God. That's when I learned that I can't depend on humans for my every need. Only God can be there for me, to meet every need I have.

I had to go to the hospital one day because I was having a panic attack, and I didn't know what it was. I thought I was having a heart attack. The doctors performed all the necessary testing and found that I had no heart problems.

The doctor asked me, "Do you want to live?" I told him I did. He said, "If you don't get your life in order, you will have a stroke or a heart attack. You have some decisions to make."

I had to make some important decisions about my life and my daughters. I went home after that conversation with my doctor and asked my husband if he would take my hand and guide me, taking over the responsibility of being a real leader of the house, almost as if I were a little child. It would just be for a little while, until I could get a grip on my emotions. That request frightened him very badly, and I knew then that I couldn't depend on him for any help. He did not pass the test.

My husband was abusing drugs; he was also having affairs with other women. He was bringing home to me sexual problems he contacted from these women, the problems was not life threatening. That was where I drew the line. I prayed to God about it. I never wanted to be a divorcee; I believe that if two Christians are married, they can work through anything. It always takes two to make it work; it can't be one-sided. I didn't know what it was like to depend on someone else for my needs and wants and provisions, but I was willing to take a chance on my husband to meet those needs.

I realized that it was too much for him. I had to fend for myself. The things I was asking my husband for; are the same things he wanted from me. I talked with my husband on a Saturday night, and I told him I wanted a divorce. I never wanted to make that statement in my life, and it was devastating to me to say that word: *divorce.*

He didn't want to split up, and he asked me if God could change my mind. I told him he was a little late to bring God into the situation. He'd had opportunities earlier. When I got up the next morning to go to church, he wanted to go too, which was unusual, because he had stopped going. I said, "Oh boy, what's next?" At the end of the sermon, the pastor did an altar call. My husband went down to the front to give his life to the Lord, Finally.

I knew he was full of drama, and I didn't believe he was sincere. He just didn't want to lose the bird nest he found on the ground. I was called to the conference room where he had been taken. He had told the pastor about my asking for a divorce. The pastor asked me if I would reconsider in light of what he had just done, saying, "If he's acting, he won't be able to keep it up very long." He said I would know whether or not he is truly sincere. So I reconsidered about the divorce. I owed it to him and to myself, a chance to see if this marriage was truly God-centered.

I believe he did get caught up in what he had done. He did well for a while, but he couldn't hold out, he failed. Eventually, we did divorce. Now it was just me and God. Sometimes we have to do what is right, even when we don't feel like it. I didn't want to divorce my husband, but under the circumstances, it was the right thing to do.

As time went on, I realized that it was the right thing for me to do. Case in point: my now-ex-husband had asked me to take a trip with him to a surprise birthday party for his aunt in another state. This was his last-ditch effort for me to receive him back into my life. I pondered this request for several weeks and decided to go. The decision was based on whether or not I needed to take another look at this situation.

I prayed to God that he would show me who my husband really was, to open my eyes and ears wide. While on this trip, God did exactly that. Have you ever asked God to make something so plain that you will have no doubts? That's what God did for me. One of the things he showed me was the reason we weren't together anymore. I remembered the reason why we got divorced, because God showed me all of the things on that trip that caused the divorce in the first place.

For seven years after that, I was single. I took the time to find out who I am and what my purpose here on Earth is. What is my spiritual gift, and how do I find out? I had a lot of questions that needed to be answered, because I wanted to be the best I could be in Jesus Christ. I needed healing in my body, in my emotions, and in my mind. If I could find healing in those areas, I would be considered a person who is well. I would probably attract a well man, if I wanted another one.

So, for seven years, I was working on myself. I was willing to let God change me into who I am supposed to be. I was changing my self-perception too. I didn't like or loved myself enough, in my opinion.

CHAPTER 13

A COWORKER AND her husband introduced me to a man they thought would be compatible with me. In the seven years following my divorce, I never dated, never had any interest in men. I was just interested in me. I didn't want to be bothered with any male outside of my family. But I agreed to meet this man, thinking, *right about now, I am probably almost well, so I'll give it a try.* I believe this was a Super Bowl Sunday. I was cooking lunch for this meeting, which took place after church.

When they arrived, I was watching them as they got out of the car—focused on the man. As I looked at him, I formed an opinion, or should I say a thought went through my mind regarding him. I kept that thought to myself and told no one. He seemed like an interesting fellow, and we agreed to have lunch one day. He invited me to attend church with him on Sunday, and I did. The pastor of the church had a message that really inspired me.

Occasionally, after that, I would visit his church. This man and I continued to see each other for about two years. I thought he was a godly man, because he was not pressuring me for sex. He was a recovering alcoholic. When I prayed, I asked God, "Please don't allow me to make another mistake." That was stupid. God gives us free will, but he shows us warnings and red flags.

God did give me warnings, but I ignored them, and I married this man. I moved my membership to his church before we were married, and the pastor of that church married us. Our wedding gift from my brother: a weekend stay at the Marriott Hotel. My husband invited his daughter on our honeymoon weekend. I was stunned. I had been celibate all those years, and I wanted no distractions on my wedding night.

I really didn't know how to handle this situation. I was at a loss for words, unsure what to do or say. His daughter went with us to the Marriott. That night, I put on a cute little outfit, waiting for my husband to come to bed—not knowing that he was waiting for me to fall asleep before he came to bed. We did not consummate the marriage that weekend. We all came back to the house and entertained the daughter, because she was from another state. We showed her the sights of our city, and then she went home.

Months passed with no consummation of the marriage. By this time, I was confused and dumbfounded. I didn't know what to make of this. This is one of the things that married people do, and I was married now, so why couldn't I get any? I asked him what the problem was, and he stated that the medication he was taking was causing him a problem. I didn't remember him telling me he was on any type of medication before we were married.

I'm not quite sure when we tried to consummate the marriage, but we finally did attempt to do this. I had fallen a few steps back to where I came from in my thoughts, my emotions, and my mental state. I was believing that it was my entire fault, that I wasn't attractive enough for him or he was just not into me. *But then why did he marry me?*

I was turning all of this inward, thinking less of myself, actually beating up on myself. I thought, *If you don't want to touch me or show any signs of affection, then it must be me that is causing this problem.* We went to church every Sunday and we were both deacons in the deacon ministry; also small-group leaders. I was also in the hospitality ministry, very active in the church. Despite all of this, I was very miserable, very depressed, very stressed. I am a believer, a follower of Jesus Christ, but I felt no victory in my life, only a lack of fulfillment.

I decided to see if I could get some help with this problem. I walked the road almost every day, talking to God, which was my form of exercise, and spending time with God. I called the church to set up a meeting with the first lady. We were in our third year of marriage when I decided to do this. Just before I made the appointment, we left church one Sunday and stopped at a grocery store. My husband went in and I stayed in the car, and I lost it. I started crying, screaming, and hollering at the top of my voice. The explosion out of my throat was so strong that it felt inflamed afterward. It offered a little release from total frustration. I was a hot mess, and I felt like I was losing my mind again.

That's when I decided I needed to talk to someone. I couldn't carry this inside me any longer without getting it out on the table; it was eating me from the inside out. I went to the appointment with the first lady and told her what was going on. She asked me how I dealt with this, and for so long. I told her it was God that kept me.

Based on that appointment, we decided we probably needed to bring in the pastor. There may have been a medical problem, or maybe my husband needed to change the medication he was taking. We set up an appointment for my husband and me to see the pastor. I went home and told my husband what I had done, asking him, "Would you be willing to go to this appointment?"

He was not happy about this. He said, "I need to tell you something before you find it out in the pastor's office." I said, I am listening, and he said that he was HIV-positive.

I surprised him by responding with sympathy and caring. I got up from my seat and went over to give him a hug. "You poor baby. I am so sorry. How long have you known?"

He told me he found out right after we were married. I was very glad to learn that the reason he would not have sex with me was because he was protecting me from being infected.

We didn't go to the appointment with the pastor, because now I knew why we hadn't been intimate with each other sexually. Then it hit me: *I need to be tested. We have lived together for three years, we have kissed, we have attempted intercourse several times.* At the time, he used a condom. I had asked why, and he said it stimulated him more. What did I know? Nothing!

I went to get tested, but I needed to know right away, not in two weeks. So I was given a twenty-four-hour test; that was a stressful twenty-four hours. I received the results, which were negative, but I needed to go back in six months to be retested. I went back after that time, and it was negative again. In fact, I went back every year for eight more years to be tested. The nurse told me I didn't have to come back anymore after the second time unless I was sexually active with someone who could be at risk. Actually, I was doing it for my own peace of mind.

I lived with my husband for three more years after learning about his condition. In that time, I went to several biblical counselors and secular counselors, trying to sort out what to do. Here I was again, facing the prospect of another divorce, which I told myself I wouldn't do, yet it seemed to be here again—another decision that would change my life.

I felt like I was living and being directed by crises in my life, like I was just waiting for the next crisis. I asked my husband if there was anything else he wasn't telling me that I needed to know. He said no, but I found out later that he lied. I went to a doctor's appointment with him, and I asked the doctor when had he; begun treating my husband for his condition. The doctor gave me a date that was two years *before* we were married. There were other things going on that could have affected me but nothing life-threatening.

My husband said he knew I wouldn't have married him if I had known about his HIV. Damn straight! With that, I realized I wasn't well yet; I was still living in the madness of the behavior I was used to. I am not an alcoholic, but I keep marrying people with substance-abuse problems. How do I disconnect from my learned childhood behavior?

Now I was feeling like a hypocrite in my church. I no longer felt that I should be part of the deacon ministry, because I was getting ready to leave my husband. I wasn't going to sacrifice my life to be with this man anymore. He lied by not telling me his problems; he didn't give me the chance to decide my fate; he made the decision for me. The marriage covenant was now null and void.

After he told me about his condition and I was relieved that I was not the cause of our problems, he was also relieved that he didn't have to carry this secret around anymore. Though we were both relieved, things were not getting any better. He still continually did things that adversely affected my life and changed who I was. I never really said a lot to my husbands about how they were making me feel; I kept it all on the inside, which was eating me up inside. One husband thought I was very passive and meek. Neither man really knew me; actually, I didn't know *myself* at that time.

You learn a lot about a person from what they say, and I didn't say much at all. I found myself using a lot of energy just to stay sane. I learned later that meekness is simply power under control. Not realizing this at that time, I would listen and watch their behavior; knowing that they were actually hanging themselves.

In the three years I lived with my second husband after finding out about his HIV, I really didn't know what to do. I had made so many wrong decisions that I was afraid to make any more. I wasn't sleeping very well; in fact, I hadn't had a good night's sleep since my first husband committed suicide. This was bringing me down physically, mentally, and emotionally. I needed to connect with the actual root of all of my problems that I had created for myself. I know I had chopped some of the top off that root, but I had not actually pulled it out. That's what I needed to do to live victoriously.

Things were stacking up on each other, and I couldn't see light. It was as if I was in the wilderness and I couldn't see my way out of the woods. I am trying to convince myself that I am fine, but I am not fine. I am tormented, and my wounds are bleeding. I am being robbed of my energy, I have no peace, and I need sleep. I made the decision to go searching for this root that was growing inside of me.

CHAPTER 14

I DIVORCED MY third husband, and hurting more than with the first divorce. I was betrayed, and I couldn't think of anything at that time that could come close to the feeling. I threw myself into my job and my church. I was on a mission to be the best I could be in Christ Jesus. I continued to be active in my church and studied the Bible. I badly needed peace and joy. I wanted to live. I was good at helping other people with their problems; it was natural for me, and I loved it. Yet I was inadequate in helping myself.

I was encouraged to attend biblical counseling classes at my church, and I did. I loved those classes, I was given the opportunity to council people professionally, I was already counseling friends and coworkers. I didn't complete the last part of the course; I bought all the books for the course, and didn't get to use them. My dad was very sick, and dying. My dad came to live with me until he died. I had too much on my plate to finish the course; I had to take care of him, and work. I asked God for a new beginning, and I asked him to restore what had been taken from me. It seemed as if God was leading me back to Texas, but I didn't want to hear that. I really never wanted to live in Texas again. I had left Texas when I was twenty years old, and I felt like that was enough years in Texas.

To confirm what I felt God was telling me, I took a trip to Texas to visit my brother, hoping to get more clarity about what I was sensing from the Lord. One day, before I left for Texas, my mind went back to my early childhood. I don't remember being a happy little girl. I was not carefree, with no responsibilities other than just to play. I still want to know what that feels like. That was taken away from me.

I wanted to experience being a little girl, free from chains that held me captive all those years ago. I could see myself in my mind's eye, running, shouting, laughing, smiling, and jumping up and down with my friends. What a wonderful feeling this must be, just to be free! I went to Texas at the end of 2003. I was really enjoying being away from the familiar as I sat on my brother's back porch, having my devotion. As I read the Bible, praying and singing songs of praise, I noticed, to my surprise, that tears were running down my face. I looked out into the yard and saw a little rabbit and a beautiful rooster. I noticed that my body was very relaxed, and I cried out to God, "If this is where you want me to be in this phase of my life, I will be obedient!"

God wanted me back in Texas. I surrendered and was submissive to my God that morning. I didn't want to resist the Lord anymore, so I gave up. Have you ever thought about whether you are allowing God to guide and control your life? I thought I was doing that, but I wasn't. Not until that moment did I realize that I was only letting God have *part* of my life. But now I was giving it all over to him, knowing that I had been making a mess of my life through my decisions.

Now that I had my answer, what was my next move? I was still working, I owned my home, loved my church, and was growing and being fed there. I went back to Washington State, put my house up for sale, and put in my papers to retire from my job. Returning to Washington State, I thought, *everything will fall in place like I think it should.* I learned that there are sequential steps that have to be taken.

I found a Realtor, and we had set a selling price for the house, made up flyers, and posted on the Realtor's website. I thought I was good to go, but it didn't work out that way. God wanted me to learn some things before he made it happen. The house had three bedrooms and a two-car garage. I had changed the garage into a family room and another bedroom. The house was not selling because people wanted a garage, so I had to convert the rooms back to a garage. I didn't really have the money to do that, so I prayed to God to bless me with the money to complete it.

I had mentioned to a friend about my dilemma, and she said she would pray with me about this. One morning, I came into work, and she said God had told her to lend me the money to convert the rooms back to a garage. I was stunned to hear this, and I praised God. He had put everyone in my life that was needed to make this move happen with ease. A young man was recommended for the conversion, and I hired him. He was very helpful, not just in converting the rooms, but also in painting them. He was a god sent. He did all the repairs that were needed; not major repairs, just tightening up a few things.

It took a year for the house to sell, and in that year, I was taught patience. God told me that it is in his timing, not mine. My nephew and his uncle drove all my possessions to Texas, including my car. My brother who was living in Texas had found a storage place for my things. I flew down later.

In that year, while waiting for the house to sell, I was communicating with people about buying a mobile home to set on the land we owned. That is where my brother was living, so we would be next-door neighbors. After all of this had taken place, my things had arrived in Texas and were now in storage. My car was sitting in my brother's yard, and I needed to go and have my new beginning in life.

My mother wanted to come to Texas with me; she said she wanted to visit her son and help me if I needed help. We arrived in Texas September 26, 2004. After arriving, I had to start looking for a home, because the person I was dealing with in Texas did not have the house I wanted. He did have a house, but it was not to my liking. One day, during my search, I passed a lot filled with mobile homes. I was told to turn around and go back to that place, and I said, "Why?" I didn't like the name of the business. But I was obedient; I turned and went back to the lot.

I looked around; all of the homes were bigger than the house I had sold in Washington State. So I came back to my brother's house to ponder; I was living with my brother and his wife until I purchased a home, which was a blessing. I told my mom about one home I looked at and described it to her. She wanted to see it, so we went to look at it. She loved it, and she pointed out to me all of the positive things I hadn't noticed.

It had four bedrooms. My plan was to downsize, rather than go bigger, because it would just be me living in this big house. I didn't want to live alone in a big house. I approached the seller and asked the cost of the house, and they made me an offer I couldn't refuse. I purchased the house and moved into my new home before Thanksgiving of that year. My mother went back home to Washington State.

CHAPTER 15

I WAS STARTING to feel peace, which I was not used to, so I asked God to help me to deal with this new feeling. Two or three months later, my mom called and said, "I believe God is leading me back to Texas also." That statement made me think, *she wants to follow me.* Remember, ever since I was a little girl, she had programmed me to take care of her; this was my responsibility to her. I was upset at this.

She wanted me to find her a senior citizens' community, and I did that for her. She didn't ask to move in with me, which I truly believe was what she wanted. Instead she was waiting for me to invite her to move in with me. With all the other trials and tribulations I had gone through, this felt like another trap to take my freedom from me. I was still trying to adjust to this new feeling of peace.

My mom moved down to Texas and into her new senior citizens' community. She is constantly saying she wanted to live on our land in the rural area, where she could have flowers, plant gardens, and play in the dirt. She loved these sorts of activities.

I found out several years later why she actually wanted me to buy that house: she wanted to live in it. She never asked to move in, but she insinuated it by telling me she could help me with my finances. I made no comment on the subject. When she left Washington State, she was living with my sister, who was not the one programmed to take care of her for the rest of her life.

So I am back in Texas where I started from; I have made a full circle. My mom was back in Texas. The question is; how will this affect my life? God, help me to comprehend what is happening now in my life. I am trying to be free to be me and have the time and the peace to hear from God what my purpose in life is.

I considered this a major distraction; the enemy was using my mom to hinder me. He is a liar, and I will not receive what he is trying to do to me. I helped my mother by paying bills for her, taking her shopping, and to doctor's appointments. Anything else that she needed, I was there to help her, but I knew what she wanted most of all was to move in with me. She whined enough to my brother until he decided he wanted her to come and live with him and his wife.

That didn't go too well, so she ended up leaving their place, to live in another place I found for her. That place didn't work out too well either, so my brother and I convinced her to live in an assisted-living facility. She went reluctantly. With my brother and me working every day, she needed to be around people, interact with people, and also get all of her needs met.

By this time, I had remarried, which did not go over well with her, because I had chosen my husband over her; I was told. So now she was angry with me, knowing now she couldn't control me. She told me once that I was too independent, which I took to mean I couldn't be persuaded by what she wanted anymore. She really didn't want to attend my wedding, which was all right with me, because my wedding was about me, not about her. My family was very late; they almost missed the wedding. My thought was, *It is what it is; move on.*

I had to convince my husband to move from his hometown to mine and move into my place. He was very stubborn about this; he felt as a man, he needed to get a place or that we get a place together. I told him it didn't make sense to do that at our age when we already had a place to live. He finally gave in because it made sense.

That was another problem with my mom: she didn't want to make it easy for me in this matter, because my husband had taken her space. I really don't know if she ever came to grips with that. In reading this, one might think that I didn't love my mother. That is not true; I adored my mother. It doesn't change the fact that everything I have said is true; my siblings would probably have different stories to tell about their upbringing and their relationship with our mother.

This is not about their life; it is about me and my life as I experienced it, felt it, and acted on it. I had to realize that mothers and fathers are people too; they have the same emotions, desires, and experiences as their children have. Most of us come from a dysfunctional family, whatever *dysfunctional* means in this sense. We all have trials and tribulations and drama in our families. It is left up to each individual to rise above what has hindered them for years. You are responsible for your own life.

My mother gave me better treatment than she received from her mother; she could only give me what she had to give and nothing more. God chose her and my dad to be my parents on purpose. I am not an accident or a "by-chance" daughter of theirs. My parents are precious to me because God chose them; he could have used anyone, but he used those two people, and from them, God knew that I would inherit something that can be used to glorify, edify, and please him. He has a purpose for my life; he has deposited in me gifts and talents, and he is using me.

CHAPTER 16

NOW I WANT to talk about the last thing that I held against my mom. Writing this is really helping me heal from bondage that has held me back from some things in my life. I am very glad that God has given me the wisdom to know this. I resented my mom. If we want freedom and healing from our open wounds, we have to admit and tell the truth. I don't like saying it, and I didn't like feeling it, but it's true. I resented her because she wouldn't let me go. She was still trying to make me responsible for her, and I didn't want to be responsible for her. I needed a chance to be responsible for myself, and it seemed like she was not going to let this happen.

I suffered with this resentment of my mother. I did a lot of crying and praying about it, knowing that it was a hindrance in my life. I wanted to be free; I didn't want my peace disturbed over this matter. So I asked God for direction on how to do this. I put an empty chair in front of me, and I talked to the chair with my invisible mother sitting in it. I told her all the things I felt she had done to me, how she made me feel, and how she didn't make me feel. I said, "I forgive you, Mom, because you did not know what you were doing to me, and I love you with all my being."

My mother lived in the assisted-living facility for a little over a year. She didn't like it at all; she would rather have been out in the rural area with my brother and me. She wanted to help my brother with his garden and my sister-in-law with her flowers. So now I had a dilemma: do I finally move her in with me and my husband? She was becoming sicker as time went by, but I still didn't get the confirmation from the Lord, and I was seeking this answer as to what to do. *Do I bring her into my home?* My life would not be my own anymore. I would be unhappy; I knew this without a shadow of a doubt.

I had finally convinced myself that the Lord had made it plain; I already knew the answer to this question. I was getting ready to mess up God's plan and ask my mother to move in with my husband and me. I know that I can't actually mess up God's plan, but I could get ahead of God and mess up the plan he had for me at that time in my life. I needed to be still.

One day when I was visiting her, she told me my brother had asked her to move back in with them for a second time, I asked her what her answer was, and she said yes. She seemed happy with that, which in turn made me happy also, for her and for me. God always has a plan. I don't know if my mother had forgiven me for not letting her live with me, but I do know that she realized there were other people in my life, and she couldn't dominate me. I lived right next door to my mom, so we could visit anytime we wanted to.

After she moved back in with my brother, she visited me only three times in three years. I would sometimes take her to her doctor appointments; she'd sit on the porch and wait for me to get ready, but she wouldn't come inside the house. It is what it is, and that was something she had to deal with it, not me.

During the last two years of her life, we laughed together a lot. She was a joy to me. Several years ago, I was thinking about how God had blessed me to forgive my mother. I start wondering what else was happening inside of me that could be hindering me from my walk with the Lord.

CHAPTER 17

A FRIEND TOLD me about a deliverance ministry; she knew I would be interested in that, because I had dealt with demons I prayed out of my house in Washington. Several ladies from the intercessory prayer ministry from my Church came over to help me, pray and cast out the demons that were left in the house after my first husband died. God enabled me, to take back my home. The Deacons that had prayed in my home several years earlier wasn't able to cast them out. I made an appointment with the ministry. I went to my appointment not knowing what to expect, knowing only that I am the righteousness of God in Christ Jesus, and no weapon formed against me shall prosper.

What an experience I had in that deliverance! All churches should have a deliverance ministry; God wants his people free. Satan keeps a lot of people in the dark, because he tells lies. He hides in your mind and suggests all sorts of things to keep us in bondage, not enjoying our everyday life.

During the deliverance, the demons started making my head hurt. I had never felt pain in my head like that before. My body started jerking; the demons were actually talking through me to the person assisting me in the deliverance. We were all talking, and the demons had to obey what was said, because it was all done in Jesus' name, the shed blood of Jesus. The demons had no choice but to obey. They were trying to hide. If we want to be free, we have to be persistent and cast them out by telling them to go into the pit of hell.

We give the enemy permission to come into our bodies, not knowing what we're doing. We open the doors several ways: through unforgiveness, anger, and bitterness. I had opened the door for the enemy to come in through these emotions. The enemy can also come into our bodies and souls through our parents from generational curses. When we rid the demons from our ancestors, they cannot come back, but we can let them back in our lives through our own behavior.

It took about two hours to finish the deliverance. When it was over, I had a feeling I can't even express completely with words. What I can say is that I felt like I had taken a shower on the inside of me. I felt clean, fresh, and cool on the inside. I still don't have words for everything that happened and is still happening to me. I do know that I don't grow in the Lord from everything being easy. We have to go through something to get something and to be the best that we can be. I have to count it all as joy, because my life can be a message to others. Only as high as I reach can I grow; only as far as I seek can I go; only as deep as I look can I see; only as much as I dream can I be.

God is still shaping and molding me, maturing me as I grow in the knowledge of him. God's Word says that he knew me before the foundation of the world, so he knew what I would go through, all the mistakes I have made and the wrong choices. I wouldn't be the person I am today without the shaping of God in my life.

I love and like myself now. There was a time when I did not like myself; I spoke curses over my life, not even knowing that I was doing so. Words are very powerful. I have learned that God's words that I receive in my mind and speak out of my mouth can become a force, releasing God's ability within me. I remember years ago, I used to make statements like, "I am going to speak this into existence," not realizing that's what I was actually doing. Whether you're speaking positive or negative things over your life, if you believe it with all your heart, you will have what you say (Mark 11:23-24). I know this from experience. I heard a statement the other day: "I am afraid of the greatness in me." That statement affected me to the point of tears, and I asked God why this statement affected me so much.

I believe all of us have greatness within us. Do we want to admit this? Can we wrap our minds around it? I don't believe God has brought me this far only to take me back again. I am running this race in my life in my own lane, reaching for what's ahead of me and saying my past is finished. I have a cloud of witnesses watching me; I need to be worthy of their attention. I want to express the highest expression of myself. My power is not where I am but where I have been. I want to live my life on purpose, and I want to run with people who are as hungry as I am. I know my identity now.

Thank God for mercy and grace.

CHAPTER 18

I FEEL I need to recap some of my life; to see how far I have come.

I didn't want to die in the environment I came from without living. I wanted a new mind-set; I wanted to grow higher than the environment I was born in. I didn't get to pick my family or their personality. I learned that it was what I was made of at that time. I was shaped by my family's environment. I wanted to see a different view of the world; I didn't like what I saw as a child growing up. I wanted peace!

I was outgrowing my hometown in my mind-set, thinking, *I am bigger than my environment. Why am I thinking differently from my friends and my expectations?* God enabled to me to leave my familiar environment and go to another environment, which almost took me out, but God had *and has* a plan for my life. I felt like God needed me to get out of my familiar environment, to shape me for his plan. My past decisions were my shaping from God for my life.

God knew that my mom and my dad possessed exactly the right genetic makeup to make me the model God had in mind. I read a book that said our parents had the DNA God wanted in order to make us. God used all of my painful experiences to shape me, preparing me for ministry; God never wastes a hurt. I heard a pastor remark one day, "Nothing I have been through was wasted."

I believe God wants me to share my painful experiences so he can use them to help others. God has shaped my personality. There never has been and never will be anybody like me. I had to discover this. I learned from God that I am special and I have a purpose. I am still discovering the spiritual gifts and abilities God has deposited in me. He is setting me free from chains that bind me, equipping me to do what he wants me to do. Each day I live with expectation; each day is new. I am excited about what God has for me every day.

God has blessed me to forgive and to recognize that some things are finished; they have no more use in my life. He has blessed me with the hunger and thirst to renew my mind in his Word, and I willingly let him lead my life. This is not always easy, because of spiritual warfare.

Being a parent is the biggest responsibility a person can have. We hold our children's lives in our hands—their future, their entire being. Some of us are failing miserably. I used to say when I was growing up that I would be a better parent than my parents. I was better in some ways, but I missed the mark. I love my daughters with a passion; they are a product of me. I loved that feeling. I had a feeling of empowerment, that God would choose me to be their mother. For him to bless me this way was awesome. Little did I know the responsibilities were so great, including provisions, protecting, loving, caring and developing their minds, their emotions, and their bodies, and doing it God's way. How do I do this when I am skating on thin ice myself?

Some parents, but not all of us, want to put our best foot forward. We want our kids to see no wrong in us, almost like we never make a mistake, like we are "holier than thou." I didn't want my kids to know I was a screw-up. My desire was to be a very good example for them, better than what I had received. But I came off, as being "picture-perfect." I believe I failed them in their emotional and mental health. The provisions, protecting and loving them, was no problem. Showing love was providing those things for them. I didn't know how to develop their mental and emotional health, because I had no tools. I needed help in those two areas of my life.

I gave everything I had to them, and I believe I failed as a parent in those areas. I couldn't give what I didn't have. Four years ago, I asked my daughters to forgive me for anything I had done that hindered their lives during their upbringing. If their dad were alive, I'm pretty sure he would ask for forgiveness also. My hope is that when my daughters read this book, it will help them in their lives, and also help them to know me better, based on my past.

My hope is that whoever reads this book will be encouraged, inspired, and motivated to live with the freedom to be who God has created you to be for the purpose of being here on Earth. Do you want to be free from the chains that bind you? If so, go searching, and ask God to show you your root problem (where it starts). Pull it out, leaving nothing, so it won't be able to grow back. Throw yourself at the foot of God's throne and say, "I give up. Please take over my life. Lead and guide me through this physical world you have put me in. I am willing to be an instrument for you to use and to show the world you are the almighty, all-knowing God, who reigns with power and love."

When we are free, we do better, because we know better. Let's know, and do better, so we can give this physical world better children and in turn better adults.

CHAPTER 19

GOD TRANSFORMED ME through troubles; he had a purpose behind every problem I had. He used my trials and tribulations to develop my character. I read a book once that stated that God depends more on circumstances to make me like Jesus than he depends on my reading the Bible. The reason is obvious: I face circumstances twenty-four hours a day (2 Corinthians 4:17). Spiritual growth is not automatic; it takes an intentional want. I wanted to grow, I decided to grow, I made an effort to grow, and I persist in growing. There's always a decision to make.

To be like Christ, you have to decide to start the process of becoming like him. I learned years ago that the way I think determines how I feel, and the way I feel influences the way I act. I am learning that feelings can betray you. Do the right thing, even if you don't feel like doing it. I can think myself happy; I can sing myself happy and have peace if I choose to (Romans 12:2). I am being transformed by truth.

The author of the book *The Purpose-Driven Life* said; that truth will transform you (Matthew 4:4). Spiritual growth is the process of replacing lies with truth (John 17:17). When God speaks, things change. My painful experiences occurred when I based my choices on unreliable authorities: culture (everybody is doing it), tradition (we've always done it), reason (it seems logical), or emotion (it felt right). I chose the Bible as my final authority.

I had to memorize Scripture to help resist temptations, reduce stress, build confidence, offer good advice, and share my faith with others. I learned to meditate, which is focused thinking. I had to focus on God's Word over and over again. It kept me sane. I knew too well how to worry, so I switched up what I was thinking. I started thinking about God's Word, not negative things. The truth will set you free. I didn't like truth right away; the truth of God's Word exposes my motives, my faults, and my sins, and I needed to change.

Applying God's Word is not easy. I had to learn to share things with other; I held the secrets and the personal hurts. The church I attended had small Bible-study groups; it was there I started opening up. Listening to other people's truths helped me a lot. That is one of the reasons I believe Bible study is vital to some people, in more ways than one.

The Bible was not given to increase our knowledge but to change our lives. Ecclesiastes 3:1 says that everything on Earth has its own time and its own season. Philippians 1:6 says, "I am sure that God who began the good work within you would keep right on helping you grow in his grace until his task within you is finally finished on that day when Jesus Christ returns." There are no shortcuts to maturity. It has taken me years to grow into any likeness of Christ; the development of Christ can be slow. Character can't be rushed; it takes time. I get very tired sometimes, but I won't hinder the process. I want my fruit to continue to grow.

What I say is evidence of what I believe. If God said it (I can do it), I believe it (I will do it), and I act on it (I must do it). My prayer is that my life can be a message to someone. May God bless you.

DECISIONS MADE TODAY FOR TOMORROW

I HAVE THE opportunity to input more of my life into this book I wrote several years ago. My desire is to inspire you, and give you food for thought, that will add to your life. Please keep reading to the very end. I am sharing some of my life with you, my past and present decisions that have and will affect my future.

I will be recapping some of the book. Growing up in Texas is where God wanted me to be, I didn't get to choose where I was to grow up or to go to school not even my parents; God chose my parents. So I had to make the best of it. Texas was dealt to me.

Being the oldest I had some advantages I could set good examples for my siblings by being honest, giving, helping others, and loving. I added to the family by learning how to drive a car with a stick, I believe it is called a standard shift. I knew how to cook, cleaned the house in essence I learned how to make do with what I had, I appreciated so much that I can function in whatever situation I'm in. I learned not to panic when I didn't have what I needed. I learn to make a way for it to happen with God's help first.

I appreciate where I came from it helps me to value and appreciate things and people. When I look back over my life I can see God drawing me to him, I was so curious about God, and I had a hunger and thirst for him, I still do, I had a desperate need for love and acceptance. I needed to be validated, it is a big deal if you don't get it and I didn't get it.

This part of the book is a follow-up of my life moving back to Texas. I moved back in September of 2004, this was to be a new beginning I married my classmate in 2007 after being back in Texas three years. We started elementary school together when we were six years old. We graduated high school together. After graduation the class went their separate ways. Some went to college some went to the Armed Forces, I joined the Air Force. Pass the test to enlist, took the physical exam I passed every exam. I wanted to be a nurse, I thought I could get schooling from the service, and I thought this was my gift from God. I had been nursing people all my life. I found out later in life that the nursing was from being an enabler.

I decided not to go into the Air Force; it was taking too long to go to basic training I was impatient I wanted to just get on with my life. I left the state of Texas in March of 1967 from Fort Worth Texas, I live there about one year and a half. From time to time I would see my husband (classmate) at class reunions, it was good seeing him at that time I had no interest in him other than he was my friend and brother in Christ.

After moving back we would talk on the phone go out to dinner he invited me to visit his church we both were divorced I knew his siblings his parents everything was familiar they were not strangers to me. I felt safe in this relationship we were the same age only three months apart.

He lived in an apartment in a town about 30 miles from Jacksonville I owed my home when we got married. We were 60 years old and we thought we would get married again, it seemed right for us at this age we would grow older together. I could tell initially he needed some help with finances from the breakup from his previous marriage. I was thinking here I go again enabling this man. Didn't want to think he was using me. Actually we might been using each other, he needed help with paying bills, I wanted to experience what it was like to be married to a godly man, safe and protected. I was disappointed when I didn't get that experience.

He retired from his job in 2011 he worked about 35 to 40 miles away from Jacksonville, I had a more economical car to drive those miles a day so I suggest we swap cars, my husband smoked cigarettes I didn't smoke my car was clean, please don't smoking in my car. He smoked in the car burned holes in the new seats and never said a word about it. I took good care of his car because it belongs to him. I was extra careful with his possession one day I looked in my little car to get something the smell was so bad from smoking I was coughing. I asked him why he did it he said you knew I smoked before you suggested to change cars; he never apologized for the damages. I never forgot how his attitude made me feel.

One morning he backed into a tree in the yard before going to work he said he didn't realize that he was steering the wrong way. I think the reason I am mentioning these things is to share the pain I was feeling each time something occurred. It was building up I was trying to get better and complete healing from my previous struggles, this is such a hindrance. He didn't want to be the man of the house because it was not his house. I kept telling him he was the man of the house. I found out it was an excuse to not do things around the house and when he tried he would do it incorrectly.

My husband worked at his job so much that he never became a handyman around the house, which is okay just admit it. I got my feelings hurt so many times I was getting depressed all over again, I was lonely a lot he didn't have a conversation, he didn't like to talk or maybe he didn't have anything to say. He loved to drink beer, and smoke black & mild cigars. After work every day until bedtime. When he retired he would start drinking in the morning, and all day and half the night constantly so I'm experiencing the same old stuff all over again. I am pretty sure my husband's drinking problem was not all from habit that turned into addiction. There is always a root that starts the habit going. He did not share that much of his life, however he shared enough for me to come to the conclusion that there was a deep root that never got removed, which happens to most of us.

Now I want to add my two daughters into the mix, my oldest daughter came to Texas she and her youngest son. Being a parent is a life sentence, I don't mean that in a negative way it is just a fact, you never stop being a parent until you are dead. My grandson went back to the Northwest when he was 14 years old to live with his dad and finish school. He could not get the hang of Texas too many yes and no ma'am and no sirs.

My daughter is now alone, which is not normal for her. She is doing things that are not the norm, dealing with people she should not be dealing with in my opinion. One day a marijuana cannabis butt was found in her backpack, she went on vacation that is what she calls it. The state she grew up in Washington State, that was legal but not in Texas, she was on vacation for several months. I've been praying for her because she's still had problems dealing with the suicide of her dad, people that commit suicide don't realize how it affect the people that they leave behind. I believe this vacation is what God ordered she needed a time out I believe God orchestrated this vacation he wanted her attention and he got it.

Her sons were crushed. I had to convey to them that she would be fine she will come back a new woman, and she did. She was awakened by God. God answered my prayer pertaining to her struggles she is growing so in the Lord, praise God for that. My second daughter I believe has genetic problems from her dad, but she will not admit it or get help. In the meantime I'm learning to cast all my cares on God, is it easy? No! It is a process. I gave both daughters to God I trust him and relied on him to take care of them. I needed to rest in his promises. I need to survive.

My husband is now drinking 12 or more 16 ounce beers every day it seems like I'm losing my grip I'm having panic attacks and rapid heartbeats and no sleep again. I started attending behavior health sessions, the therapist figured out I still had some residue of my first husband still in my life, I am talking 40 years ago, she was right I was still angry that he left like he did, he left me do raise the girls without him so I wrote a letter of loss to him and then I burned it that really helped.

My now husband is fading away before my eyes from beer and black and mild cigars. I was grieving for him for about two years, that process is worse to me that grieving for someone that has died. I tried to help my husband with his addiction to alcohol and tobacco I didn't know why I thought I could help, I couldn't help my dad nor my other husbands they all had addictions. I was going down the drain with them. I realize with the last husband that I can support him by loving him, accepting him in his condition, try and make him content and help him with the quality of life he preferred. He was a believer in Jesus Christ, but was irresponsible towards his body his Temple. I ask God to help me to not be resentful or bitter toward my husband. I talk to him about his problem and he would always say we all have to die from something.

When I ask God to help me to deal with what I was living with he answered by giving me peace and joy to spend my days with my husband. I also realize he had his life and I had mine. I was so glad he was enjoying his everyday life especially when I was not bugging him about his behavior.

When my husband saw the change in me it freed him to enjoy his life the way he wanted to without shame, before that change in me I was a nervous wreck he had began falling to the floor often. I never knew what I would find when I heard the sound of the fall, he was not able to get up. We shared the same doctor and the doctor was trying to prepare me for the worse and one morning I found him on the floor by the bed dead, the one thing I feared might happen happened. We were married 14 years when he died. I didn't have anything to be regretful about, I didn't used the statement that some of us use when a loved one dies, the phrase I wished I coulda, woulda have done something statement. God set me free when I asked him to change my heart toward my husband by treating him like I wanted to be treated. It hurt me to see him fading away before my eyes it was not easy. I had peace because God was my source.

My husband and I enjoy each other so much before the day of loss I miss him, sometimes when I leave home and come back my husband will be waiting at the door to let me in, if I had a meeting to go to at night he would wait up for me he was a good man.

I am busy at my church I am part of the leadership ministry I am so blessed to have this church family. I am living my best days right now. I've always wanted to share my life with someone. I do like my own company.

Sometime my daughters and brothers make statements about my having four husbands I would tell them I was trying to get it right, I was kidding I had biblical reasons if I wanted to leave the marriages, I never wanted a divorce I stayed as long as I could in each.

Wrong decisions transformed me into who I am today, and then again I can say was the decisions wrong? I could look at it as a way God was shaping and molding me to get me to where I am now, because he knows how to do that.

I have an ex-husband who is still living after forgiving him for his part in my life tragedies, we talk to each other and we check on each other he is my brother in Christ. I am now trying to correct some of the damage I did to my body from all the stress, tension, anxiety, and depression that I have suffered for years.

My doctor tells me that some of my problem is my adrenal gland after a test it showed that I was flat line because of years of anxiety and stress, there was no let up it was continually. I don't know how long it would take to get me back up to speed. I am grateful for the help that God is supplying me with, God is the reason I live, moved, and have my being. I have to remember I am dealing with PTSD. My open wounds that were bleeding for years are closing up those are the mental and emotional wounds. I still have sometimes physical pain hits my stomach and go straight to my back, stomach produces so much acid if

I drink water it would be painful. I know who I am, and who God says I am.

My past hurts are diminishing, all of this is in God's timing, one of my thoughts are how God how long? I have to enter into his rest. Jesus has finished everything that I need to survive from the cross. The Lord created the unmerited favor to us as a people in this physical world which is grace, it is all finished, but in order to receive it you have to have enough faith to achieve it.

My desire is to share my blessings with others. In the spirit there is a whole world which joy, peace, healing, provision and favor already has been bought for me and for you, we need to see that through spiritual things we have spiritual eyes, we have physical eyes we can see with both just like physical food and spiritual food we need both to function well. I am a widow now again first time at the age of 30, now over 40 years later what a difference. God is opening my eyes daily to the truth about the overwhelming greatness of his power and love towards me. I declare that my heart is seeing more clearly every day, and what I see I believe which is faith, my latter years are much better than my former years. Praise God I can say that. I was getting a little worried it seems I wasn't getting any relief. I discovered what I was saying and believing was causing a lot of my problems. God's word always works but some words can work for or against you depending on how you apply it.

The principle of seed time and harvest the words I spoke are seeds that produced after its kind. I started speaking positive not negative words it works!! My days get brighter and lighter. I like to believe I made a difference in my husband's life physically and spiritually. He did devotions every day and prayed. I didn't see that at the beginning of the marriage. I ask God years ago to make me a living testimony for others. I hope I was a blessing to my husband I sure wanted to be. He told me that I was a tall drink of water I assume he meant I was refreshing to him.

My first husband said I was a breath of fresh air I never forgot those words that was said to me. I believe I made a difference in their lives. I was unhappy most of my life, I know others have felt the same aren't you tired of being sick and tired? I matter and I am significant. I am learning that being in this world makes a difference in the atmosphere. We all are more than what we see. What keeps me sane is the relationship I have with the Lord it is scary without him. I programmed myself and my marriage didn't realize I was doing it, each day I knew what I had to do, I thought every day, what I wanted each day, I knew what I wasn't going to get each day, that was based on history in the past. I knew each day I had never lived in that day before, because it was new. Each day I praise God for each new day.

I had expectations each day that was interesting, but I wanted more conversation, attention, words of affirmation. I wanted a husband to do things with like fishing, playing game, entertaining friends, make plans. We did worship together at church. Now that I'm a widow this is like a new beginning what do I do now? What do I say now?

Where do I go now? Who are my friends? I look out the window with a blank stare sometimes wanting to scream, but determined to hold on. The enemy is trying to control my mind. I fight each day for my mind the mind is the battle ground between me and the devil.

I pray a lot for people and myself. God brings people to my mind to pray for, he put people in my path to witness to, he gives me words to say to them, it seems I'm rambling on; this is good for me to ramble at this time for some reason. I manage to say hidden thing when I ramble. God only knows why. I have cousins, brothers, nieces, and nephews around they have their own lives. I don't bother them when I am lonely. I try not to think about the number of my age, this started happening about 12 months ago after my husband died. I don't want to be put into a box, I am unique to me, I am like no one else don't compare me to anyone.

I am in a new phase of life it would be great to share it with someone. I never had a long period of time with anyone other than my kids they are the longest relationship in my life, and my parents of course, as you can see I'm floundering right now in my life but God is my source, shield, and protector, he is my strength to endure whatever comes my way. It does help to have a human touch.

Thank you God for my church they play a big part in my life it keeps me focus on God and his people, it sometimes takes my mind off me and mine. I must say the fighting every day, I mean this spiritual warfare is very tiring I won't give up I might not look the same as before however I am a better person on the inside that matters most.

I read a book that influenced my life and it is called "The tongue A Creative Force." It is in my power to release the ability of God. I started saying the power of God is in me to put me over, greater is he that is within me then he that is in the world (1 John 4:4) I am quickened according to the word of God. I thank God that the ability of God is released within me. I stand before demons I stand before sickness and disease and I have no fear, because the ability of God is released within me by the words of my mouth and by the word of God.

It has been a blessing to be back in Texas. I believe God blesses us in certain places and at certain times so we need to be at the right place at the right time. I believe God has made a way for certain people to be in our lives to help us on this journey. There is a purpose as to why I am in Jacksonville Texas.

I have come full circle back where I was born it is humbling for me I can say God why? The progress I've made up to now is being tested, my knowledge, wisdom, sanity, understanding ability and skills, the enemy's goal is to make you doubt God and tell you lies. He will use anything and anybody to deceive you.

We as Christians need each other to watch each other's back and our circle of people we need to trust them at all times. Never run away from your problems stand, stay, and fight so you don't have to revisit the same problems over and over again, be like Barney Fife of the Andy Griffith show, he would say "nip it in the bud" the Bible says we have not because we asked not, we need to go boldly to the throne of grace and make our requests with thanksgiving do not fret or have any anxiety about anything you also want the peace that goes along with the requests.

God did not bring me out this far to leave me he has a plan for my life and he's working it out through me every day. Sometimes we don't see what God is doing…. the small blessings and mercies.

I have learned this in life, and my advice to you whoever is reading this book is to ask God for wisdom …..The quality of having experience, knowledge, and good judgment; the quality of being wise to travel in this physical world. Be adventurous….ready to take risks, deal with the new and unknown. Be somewhat challenging….testing your abilities. Be questioning and inquisitive…..If you are inquisitive that means you love to inquire; you are always asking questions. Don't become a private detective if you don't have an inquisitive personality. The old word for question is query, which you can hear in inquire, which means to ask questions. Joy filled with hope…..May the God of hope fill you with all joy and peace as you trust in him, so that you may overflow with hope by the power of the Holy Spirit (Romans 15:13). I love this song…Joy bells keep ringing in my soul, Joy bells keep ringing in my soul joy bells joy bells…Jesus keep ringing in my soul Jesus, Jesus, Jesus keep ringing in my soul. I get joy when I think about what you have done for me.

I have realized I have an open mind….my willingness to search actively for evidence against my favored beliefs, or plans, and to weigh evidence fairly when it is available. I am not wishy-washy, or incapable of thinking for myself. I do have a different perspective now compared to when I left Texas….my way of thinking about some things, especially things that is influenced by my beliefs, experiences, and city life verses small town life. Returning to a small town has caused me some struggles….mind set, language, communication, and philosophy: understanding fundamental truths about yourself, the world in which you live, and your relationships to the world and to each other. I have to remember you can only go has high as what you are exposed to. I have no regrets being back in my home town, this is where I am supposed to be at this time. God is giving me grace to function.

I hope I have said something that gives you food for thought. Something said that adds to your life if so pass it on. Writing these few pages has been a blessing for me. God bless.

Last but not least, to my three musketeers from First Christian Church, one of them no longer attends. Thank you so much for your friendship, your love, and your encouragement. I appreciate you letting me lean on you these last few years, by letting me vent and cry on your shoulders. I love you very much.

ACKNOWLEDGMENTS

IN LABORING WITH this book for over twenty years, I would like to acknowledge the following: God, thank you; I am so grateful for your love and acceptance.

To my Daughters and Grandsons, thank you for making me feel special every day of my life, without making an effort—just being.

My grandfather, John Garlington, James Martin, Rick Warren, Creflo Dollar, T.D. Jakes, and Joyce Meyer. Have all contributed to my spiritual growth. All of these men and woman have been God-sent to me. I am so thankful God put them in my path.

I have a host of sister friends I am not naming by name. They know who they are. All of you encouraged me to keep on keeping on. Thank you so much; I love you.

Last but not least, to my husband—thank you for your patience, your love, and your encouragement to finish the book. I love you very much.

ABOUT THE AUTHOR

For author Doe Running Deer, life has been a series of tragedy and healing. In My Past Decisions Have Made Me Who I Am Today, she narrates the stories of her trials and tribulations, sharing how faith helped her get through the difficult periods.

Using personal anecdotes to illustrate how God has worked in her life, she explores the doubts, fears, and perplexities she experienced and describes how she found comfort and guidance in the Bible and through prayer. In this memoir, she recalls growing up as the oldest of four in a small Texas town against the backdrop of her father's alcoholism, and parents' marital issues. being molested by a cousin at an early age; being introduced to Jesus Christ in her teenage years; marrying an alcoholic; and enduring his subsequent suicide.

With scriptural examples to highlight key points, My Past Decisions Have Made Me Who I am Today serves to communicate the message that there is healing and that God is listening and is rescuing his people from the hurt and pain.